Hello!!!

Welcome to this very special edition of *Topz*, where the Gang investigate the power and meaning of prayer!

Did you know that you can talk to God wherever and whenever you like? That's right – He is *always* listening – and He's really interested in what you have to say! Even though God knows everything already, He wants to hear what's going on in *your* world. He's the very best Father and friend – and talking and listening to Him is a great way to get to know Him.

Whether you've been praying since you were really small, or you've never prayed before – I hope this book will teach you lots about just how much God loves you, and can't wait to have a conversation with you today!

Lynette

Chatterbox
PAGE 3

Start a conversation
PAGE 6

Just talk!
PAGE 10

Prayer makes a difference
PAGE 14

Prayer problems
PAGE 16

Jesus prayed
PAGE 20

Let the Holy Spirit in
PAGE 25

Thanks!
PAGE 28

Welcome, God
PAGE 31

Answerz and how to order *Topz*
PAGE 33

MY BIBLE BOOKMARK

Topz
READING THE BIBLE

OLD TESTAMENT

- Genesis
- Exodus
- Leviticus
- Numbers
- Deuteronomy
- Joshua
- Judges
- Ruth
- 1 Samuel
- 2 Samuel
- 1 Kings
- 2 Kings
- 1 Chronicles
- 2 Chronicles
- Ezra
- Nehemiah
- Esther
- Job
- Psalms
- Proverbs
- Ecclesiastes
- Song of Songs
- Isaiah
- Jeremiah
- Lamentations
- Ezekiel
- Daniel
- Hosea
- Joel
- Amos
- Obadiah
- Jonah
- Micah
- Nahum
- Habakkuk
- Zephaniah
- Haggai
- Zechariah
- Malachi

NEW TESTAMENT

- Matthew
- Mark
- Luke
- John
- Acts
- Romans
- 1 Corinthians
- 2 Corinthians
- Galatians
- Ephesians
- Philippians
- Colossians
- 1 Thessalonians
- 2 Thessalonians
- 1 Timothy
- 2 Timothy
- Titus
- Philemon
- Hebrews
- James
- 1 Peter
- 2 Peter
- 1 John
- 2 John
- 3 John
- Jude
- Revelation

1 Cut out 'My Bible Bookmark' and use it to help you find your way through the Bible! You could also use it to keep your place in this *Topz*! (Why not stick it to a piece of card to strengthen it, too?)

2 To find a Bible reading, find the book of the Bible first (Genesis). Then find the chapter (25) and then the verses (2–5).

Genesis 25 v 2-5

Chapter   Verse

3 Try praying this before you read the verses: 'Dear God, please speak to me through these words. I'm listening. Amen.'

4 Read the verses slowly and read them a couple of times. If you don't understand a word or two, ask a parent/carer or older Christian.

To solve the puzzles in *Topz* you will need a **Good News Bible**.

Chatterbox

Are you a chatterbox? I am. Once I start chatting, I can't stop. Especially when I'm with Josie – I talk to her about anything and everything! John says I'm the only person he knows who can go on and on about nothing and make it sound as though I'm actually going on and on about something really important – which I think is a bit rude...

Mostly bikes. Or camping.

I can be a bit of a chatterbox too. But everything I say *is* really important. Mostly because it's about computers. Or go-karts.

With me, it's food.

Sarah does enough talking for both of us!

Sport for me!

I talk about TV sometimes, or music.

Do you like chatting? Write down the names of three friends you really enjoy talking to:

_____

_____

_____

But did you know there's someone else you can have a good natter to? Someone who's always ready to listen – no matter what you want to talk about – and who just wants to be involved in your life?

3

Best friend

God is the best friend you'll ever have. And He just loves to hear from you!

The Topz Gang have told you some of what they like to talk about. Use the space below to make a list of things you like to chat over with your friends. Maybe it's hobbies, holidays, books... or perhaps it's things you're worried about, such as difficult homework, or someone you know who isn't very well.

_____
_____
_____
_____
_____

Finished? Have a good look at your list. Did you know you can talk to God about everything you've written down? Every single thing! God wants to know what makes you happy and what makes you sad. He wants to hear about your good days and your bad days. So, tell Him – because God really is the best listener ever.

TOPZ TIP

Prayers don't have to be long and full of difficult words – God loves you exactly as you are, so just be yourself when you talk to Him.

God is...

When you talk to your friends on the phone, you don't have to imagine what they look like. Even though you can't see them at that moment, you can picture them because you've met them in person. No one knows what God looks like, but we do know what His character is like because the Bible tells us all about Him.

Here are some words that describe our Father God. Can you find them all in the word search?

- KIND
- PATIENT
- CREATIVE
- CARING
- FORGIVING
- WELCOMING
- LOVING
- CALM
- WONDERFUL
- GENEROUS
- WARM
- UNDERSTANDING

Answer on page 33.

```
Q P V F O K L E T L M C A L M
W P B O C P E D W F X A Q A Z
E O N R X P S B C R O R U N G
R I M G E N E R O U S I G H K
T U L I Z X R I S P V N K A Y
Y L O V I N G H R A H G T E W
L Y K I Q Y S I U T C I B R E
U T J N A R L N E I E O E T L
F R H G Z R K L S E L V P Y C
R E G F W F I S I N I P O B O
E W F C S V N T M T E A I N M
D Q D M X T D O A C B R Q I I
N S R D E G B E I O P T L A N
O A U N D E R S T A N D I N G
W S I R H C Y H N U J M I E K
```

When you talk to God, you can know exactly who is listening!

PRAY

God, thank You for all the amazing things You are. And thank You that when I talk to You, You're always ready to listen! Amen.

Start a conversation

Sarah admits she's a chatterbox! But do you know what's really annoying? When I tell her something and she *totally* ignores me. She often ignores me when she's reading or watching TV, but other times she ignores me just because she knows it winds me up! It's really frustrating talking to someone who doesn't answer – especially when they normally don't stop talking!

God never ignores us. When you talk to Him, He will always answer. Whether it feels like it or not, God is there, listening to you. He may not answer with a big, booming voice. He may not use words at all. But the minute you say something to God, you start a conversation.

I know what you're thinking: how can you have a conversation with someone who doesn't use words? But God uses different ways to let us know what He thinks and what He wants us to do, or not to do. He may use words sometimes, but they might be words you read, or words someone else says.

How does God speak to us?

Through the Bible!
The Bible teaches us so much! We can learn about...
- God and His love for all of us
- the lives of people who have been His special friends
- Jesus (God's Son) and how He has made it possible for us to talk to God anywhere, anytime, and to be with Him forever
- how to live the way God wants us to – the way that's best for us.

The Bible shows us all of these things. But did you know that God speaks to us through the Bible too – about things that are happening in our lives right now?

If you've been praying about something in particular, you may find that when you read your Bible, a verse or a story jumps out at you. When that happens, it could be God letting you know what's the best thing to do.

PRAY
God, thank You that when I talk to You, it's not just a one-way conversation. Thank You for speaking to me too. Amen.

TOPZ TIP
As you read the Bible, ask God to speak to you through it. And remember – when you talk to God, listen out for His answer. Don't forget to say 'thank You' when you hear it!

Keep listening

Here are some more ways you might hear from God...

Through your conscience
Never ignore your conscience – that little voice inside that says, 'You need to be honest and own up' or, 'How about helping out?' God can use your conscience to let you know the best thing to do.

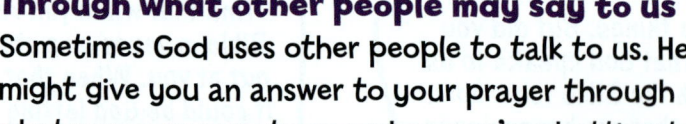

Through what other people may say to us
Sometimes God uses other people to talk to us. He might give you an answer to your prayer through what someone says to you when you're chatting to them. Or maybe, if you go to church, it could be through what a youth group leader says.

TOPZ TIP

Sometimes it's God who starts the conversation! So keep your ears (and eyes) open and stay tuned in to Him every day.

Know God's voice

God might speak to us because He wants us to do something. There is a boy at school who no one used to speak to. But in football practice once, I felt like God was asking me to invite him onto my team. I didn't want to at first, but the feeling wouldn't go away. So I asked him to play, and we got talking. He's now one of my best friends and we play football every week!

In the Bible, Jesus says He is a good shepherd to His sheep. He means that He looks out for people the way a shepherd looks out for the flock. And sheep learn to know their shepherd's voice – just as we can get to know God's.

TOPZ TIP

The more time you spend with God, talking to Him and reading the Bible, the more you'll learn to recognise His 'voice'. When God speaks, you won't want to miss it!

Follow the arrows to read what Jesus says in John 10 v 27:

'My sheep listen to my voice; I know them, and they follow me.'

Just talk!

The hardest time to talk to anyone can be when something bad or sad is happening. If things are going wrong, chatting with God might be the last thing you feel like doing.

It was like that when I thought we were going to have to move away from Holly Hill because of Dad's job. I didn't want to go! But it was hard to talk to the Gang about it because I thought they wouldn't understand. I even told myself they wouldn't miss me if I went.

Even though we definitely would have!

It was even harder to talk to God. I couldn't work out what was going on. I just wanted Him to make it all stop.

Tick the box next to the sentence that best describes you:

When I'm sad, I talk to everyone about the problem. ☐
When I'm sad, I talk to my best friend or my family. ☐
When I'm sad, I don't talk to anyone. ☐

All-weather friend

Sarah's Bible verse pick: 'Leave all your worries with him, because he cares for you.' (1 Peter 5 v 7)

GRAB YOUR BIBLE

Have you heard of a 'fair-weather' friend? It means the sort of 'friend' who likes being around when everything is going well, but seems to disappear as soon as a problem turns up.

But God is the complete opposite! He is the most amazing 'all-weather' friend you could ever have! He is there for you all the time. He wants to hear from you whether you're happy or sad, excited or bored.

PRAY

Thank You, God, for being my all-weather friend. When I don't feel like talking, please help me to talk to You anyway. Amen.

TOPZ TIP

When you're feeling down, talk to God *first* – even if He's the last person you feel like talking to. He cares more than you could possibly imagine!

In His hands

When you have problems or worries or sad feelings, know that God will:

- stay close beside you
- never leave you
- be there for you to talk to whenever you need Him
- hold your hand
- always work things out in the best possible way.

Look at the picture of the two hands below. Now imagine they are God's hands and write your name in them or draw yourself sitting in them:

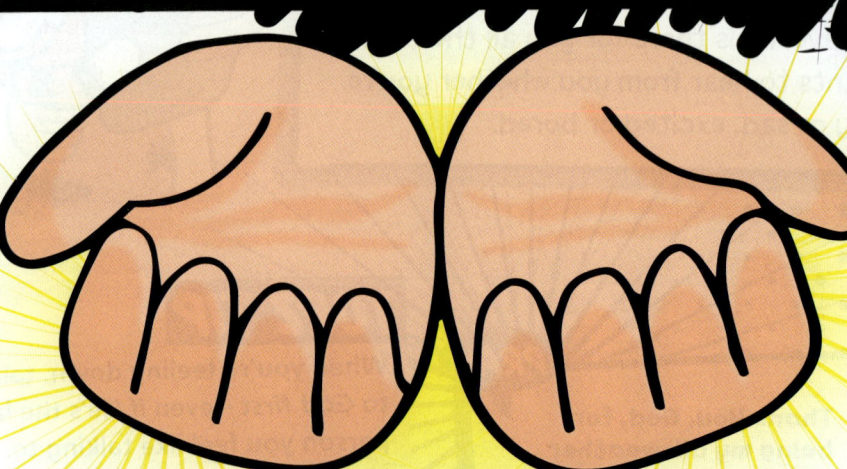

We can go to God and tell Him everything that's going on – and He holds us in His loving hands.

Be honest

People in the Bible didn't just talk to God when they were happy. Sometimes they talked to Him when they were really miserable. Or really cross! And they told Him exactly how they felt.

There was a man called Job who went through a terrible time. Everything seemed to be going wrong. In the end, he opened up to God: 'I can't be quiet! I am angry and bitter. I have to speak' (Job 7 v 11).

When there was a famine in her country, a woman called Naomi moved away with her husband and two sons. But then her husband and both her sons died. Back in her home country, she let God know exactly how miserable and let down she felt: 'When I left here, I had plenty, but the LORD has brought me back without a thing' (Ruth 1 v 21).

It can be easy to blame God when everything goes wrong. But **God doesn't make bad things happen to us.** What He does do is promise to walk beside us when we're in trouble. He wants us to be totally honest with Him about how we feel.

Prayer makes a difference

When something matters to me, I keep going on about it – like when I wanted Dad to build a go-kart with me. I just didn't stop – 'Dad, when can we start on the go-kart?... Dad, when can we drive it?'

When something's important, we keep on about it, don't we? But sometimes we give up talking to God. If we don't get an answer straightaway, we think we're not going to – or we never really believed God would answer in the first place.

Write every other letter in the read-around in the space below to find another Topz Tip from the Gang. Start at the arrow:

Answer on page 33.

START

P	A	R	B	A	C	y	D	E
N	H	O	I	P	N	Q	G	E
T	X	P	y	P	Z	R	R	R
M	E	D	N	E	G	.	A	S	F
S	W	I	C	y	B	A	S	C
L	E	V	K	U	O	T	S	G
E	K	G	J	N	I	A	H	H

_____

_____

_____

_____

The widow and the judge

It's great to read the stories Jesus told in the Bible. Here's one of my favourites. Jesus told it to get people to keep going with their prayers. He knew how much talking to God matters.

There was once a judge who didn't care about God or about people. And there was a widow who kept going to see him saying, 'Please help me. Please do what's right and fair.'

For a long time, the judge took no notice. But the widow kept on going to him and asking for help. And because she did, the judge did help her.

If a judge who didn't care helped a widow because she kept going to see him, won't God listen to and answer the prayers of the people He loves? Of course He will! And He'll answer at the right time and in the best possible way.

Why not read this story for yourself? You'll find it in Luke 18 v 1-8.

GRAB YOUR BIBLE

Prayer problems

Benny's Bible verse pick: 'The prayer of a good person has a powerful effect.' (James 5 v 16)

GRAB YOUR BIBLE

Sometimes praying can seem difficult. You might find it hard to make time to pray. Or maybe when you stop to talk to God, you realise you don't really know what to say.

I find praying tough when I'm hungry. When my stomach's empty I can't think about anything else except food!

Is there anything that makes praying difficult for you? Write it down here:

_____
_____
_____

Ask God to help you with this problem. You can be sure He will.

PRAY

I want to get closer to You, God. Please help me to talk to You every day. Amen.

TOPZ TIP

The more you pray, the closer you get to God, and the more your prayers can make a real difference!

Prayer pals

Paul's Bible verse pick: (Jesus said) 'For where two or three come together in my name, I am there with them.' (Matthew 18 v 20)

GRAB YOUR BIBLE

If you do have trouble praying, why not find a prayer pal to pray with you? They could be a Christian friend from school, or someone you see if you go to church. You could even choose more than just one person! If you're making time to meet up with a friend to pray, you're making special time to meet up with God. And listening to your friend's prayers might help you know what to say in your own prayers, too.

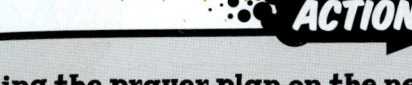

ACTION

Using the prayer plan on the next page, plan a time to pray with one or two friends this week!

My prayer plan

TOPZ TIP

To make the most of your prayer time, have a think about what you'd like to pray about, either on your own or with your prayer pal. Next, make a prayer plan so you know exactly what you're going to talk to God about each time you meet up. Then you can both pray about the things that are important to you.

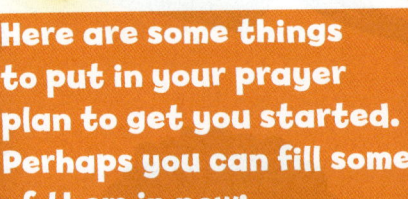

Here are some things to put in your prayer plan to get you started. Perhaps you can fill some of them in now:

My prayer pal is: _____

Day we are meeting: _____

Time we are meeting: _____

I'd like to pray about:
_____
_____

People I'd like to pray for:
_____
_____

I want to thank God for:
_____
_____

Making time

I feel like I've always got so much to do! Mum's always telling me to keep my room tidier. I say to her, 'Mum, if you didn't make me go to school, I'd have loads of time to keep my room tidy!' She says I still have to go to school though…

Finding time to talk to God on busy days can be tricky. When there are lots of things you *have* to do and things you *want* to do, praying and spending time with God can get pushed down the list.

Can you get John through the maze, avoiding the different distractions so that he can put God first?

Answer on page 33.

Jesus prayed

In the Gospels of Matthew and Luke, you can find a special prayer that Jesus spoke to teach people how to talk to God. Here it is from Luke 11 v 2-4, but some of the letters are in code.

Use the codebreaker to write out the prayer and then read Jesus' words out loud:

'F⋀thᐁr: M⋀y yᐁr h⋁ly n⋀mᐁ bᐁ

hᐁnᐁrᐁd; m⋀y yᐁr K⬜ngdᐁm

comᐁ. G⬜vᐁ ⬜s d⋀y by d⋀y thᐁ

fᐁᐁd wᐁ nᐁᐁd. Fᐁrg⬜vᐁ ⬜s ᐁur s⬜ns,

fᐁr wᐁ fᐁrg⬜vᐁ ᐁvᐁryᐁnᐁ whᐁ dᐁᐁs

⬜s wrᐁng. ⋀nd dᐁ nᐁt br⬜ng ⬜s tᐁ

h⋀rd tᐁst⬜ng.'

A guide

Jesus' special prayer includes:

1. honouring God
2. only asking for what we need
3. asking for forgiveness, and forgiving other people
4. asking to be looked after.

> Jesus' prayer reminds me what I can put into my own prayers when I'm spending time with God.

Using Jesus' words to guide you, write down what you can include in your prayers this week:

What has God done for you over the last few days that you can praise Him for?

_____
_____

Is there anything you need right now? Perhaps some help, or to be brave? Make sure it is what you need and not just what you want!

_____
_____

Is there anything you'd like to ask God to forgive you for? Is there anyone you need to forgive?

_____
_____

Do you need God to help you or look after you in a special way at the moment? Or perhaps you'd like Him to help you follow Him?

_____
_____

Follow Jesus' example

Praying to His Father God was seriously important to Jesus. In the Gospels, you can read about different times when He went off by Himself to pray...

'Very early the next morning, long before daylight, Jesus got up and left the house. He went out of the town to a lonely place, where he prayed' (Mark 1 v 35).

'After sending the people away, [Jesus] went up a hill by himself to pray' (Matthew 14 v 23).

'At that time Jesus went up a hill to pray and spent the whole night there praying to God' (Luke 6 v 12).

TOPZ TIP

Follow Jesus' example and try to make time to be with God. Whatever's going on – good things or bad things, worrying things or scary things – turn to God and pray!

Where and when?

It doesn't matter where or when you talk to God, as long as you talk to Him. Here are some of the Gang's favourite prayer times and places...

My room at bedtime. Or sometimes right after school if something's happened that I want to talk to God about as soon as I can.

I think my favourite time to pray is when I'm going somewhere in the car with Mum and Dad. I just sit in the back and talk to God in my head.

I think my best place to talk to God is in church on Sunday mornings. I like talking to Him when lots of people around me are doing the same thing.

I like talking to God in the morning when I take Gruff out for a walk.

Do you have a favourite time and place to pray?

_____
_____
_____

TOPZ TIP

If you can, try praying in different places and at different times of the day to find out what works best for you. If talking to God at bedtime means you drop off to sleep in the middle, make space at another time of day instead.

23

Prayer power

God always hears our prayers. *Always*. And He answers in the way that's best for us.

Sometimes we might not get an answer straightaway because God is saying, 'Wait.' It can be frustrating not to get an answer quickly, but it doesn't mean that God has forgotten you or that He doesn't care. It just means that now isn't quite the right time.

Remember – God knows us inside out! He knows what's best for each of us.

TOPZ TIP

Start a prayer diary! Write down things you're praying about in a notebook, and for every page you write on, leave the opposite page blank. When you get an answer, jot it down on the blank page next to the right prayer.

If you're ever feeling discouraged, have a read through your prayer diary to see how much God has done for you. It really helps!

Let the Holy Spirit in

Sarah's Bible verse pick: 'God, who sees into our hearts, knows what the thought of the Spirit is' (Romans 8 v 27)

GRAB YOUR BIBLE

Jesus lived on earth for 33 years. When He went back to heaven, His friends, the disciples, were really upset and scared. They didn't know how to cope without Him. But Jesus asked God to send a helper to them – His Holy Spirit. The Spirit would live inside them and make them brave enough to tell people about Jesus.

God sends His Holy Spirit to His friends today too. And the Holy Spirit helps us to pray. Even if we feel stuck and can't seem to find the right words to say to God, God will understand – because His Spirit will speak to Him for us. How cool is that?!

PRAY

Thank You, Holy Spirit, for living inside me to be my helper and my friend. Please help me as I talk to Jesus and God the Father so that they know exactly what I'm trying to say. Amen.

TOPZ TIP

Invite the Holy Spirit to be with you during your prayer times.

Check up

Josie's Bible verse pick: 'if we confess our sins to God... he will forgive us our sins and purify us from all our wrongdoing.' (1 John 1 v 9)

GRAB YOUR BIBLE

Does God ever feel far away when you try to talk to Him? It could be the Holy Spirit giving you a nudge to do a very important check: do you need to say sorry to God for something?

The Dixons Gang dared me to steal something once – and I did it. I felt so bad and thought that God would never want to be my friend ever again! But when I said sorry to Him, and I really, *really* meant it, it cleared everything up. It was like a big, black cloud floating away and I could chat to God again the way I could before.

TOPZ TIP

Don't let anything get in the way of your prayer times with God. Make sure you've said a genuine 'sorry' for anything you need to. Then know that God forgives you.

Other people need prayer too

The Holy Spirit is a brilliant 'nudger'! He lets you know about things in your own life that you need to talk to God about. But prayer isn't just about us. **Sometimes, God's Spirit nudges you to pray for other people too.**

You might find you're nattering away to God when, suddenly, someone pops into your head. Maybe a friend, maybe someone in your family. It could even be one of your teachers! The reason that person has suddenly showed up in your brain might be because the Holy Spirit is telling you to pray for them. Even if you don't know why or what it is they need, you can still ask God to be with them and to bless them.

When we pray for other people, we hold them up to God so that He can touch them with His love. They might need prayer because they're not well, or are having a hard time. But everyone needs prayer – because everyone needs God.

Trace over the dotted letters and colour in this Topz Tip:

REMEMBER TO PRAY FOR OTHER PEOPLE

Thanks!

Danny's Bible verse pick: 'Give thanks to the LORD, because he is good' (1 Chronicles 16 v 34)

GRAB YOUR BIBLE

Did you come up with some things to thank God for on your prayer plan on page 18? Here are some things I'm grateful to God for. Are some of these the same for you?

See if you can find all the words in the word search:

- FAMILY
- FRIENDS
- HOME
- FOOD
- WATER
- SPORT
- HOLIDAYS
- WEEKENDS
- HEALTH
- BEACH
- SUNSHINE
- SLEEP

Answer on page 33

```
H N I D R A S C O D A F W
O E A A H O L I D A Y S E
M G A S D Y E B V C X U D
E O X L I T E N M P T N E
L D E V T R P U I O R S R
O O B D R H H C R A O H F
V O E E O R D C S E P I T
A F W W E E K E N D S N G
B Q D A R H T O E G D E B
E E V T W O T F A M I L Y
A N Z E Z P Y A C S E B Y
C U F R I E N D S J K L H
H J Y R R E B Y B N I A N
```

28

A good thanking habit

"If someone gives me something – like sweets, or a birthday present, or I get invited to a party – I always say thank you. It's what you do, isn't it? But a lot of the time, somehow we forget to say thanks to God."

God made the incredible world we live in. He thought of everything: the sun to give light and warmth; rain so that plants would grow; earth and seeds so that we could sow crops and feed ourselves. All the amazing animals were put together by God too!

"And what about us? What about all the amazing things we can do... and think... and create? It's total genius! God is amazing."

Here's a prayer of thanks. Why not say it right now?

PRAY

Lord God, You are wonderful! Thank You for giving us such a fantastic planet to live on. Thank You for every day and every night. Thank You for all the creatures that share the world with me. Thank You for everything I can do and everything I am. Thank You for making me and loving me. Amen.

Satisfied

GRAB YOUR BIBLE

Dave's Bible verse pick: 'Don't worry about anything, but in all your prayers ask God for what you need, always asking him with a thankful heart.' (Philippians 4 v 6)

Sometimes people only pray when they want something. They might ask for more money, or an easy life where they don't have to work too hard! We can all go to God with a long list of things we *want* – but God wants us to be content with the things He has already given us.

If all we ever do is ask for more, we'll never be satisfied. How ever much we have, we'll always be after something else. But if we say thank You to God for everything He's given us, we'll realise how much we've already got, and stop worrying about what we think we haven't got!

TOPZ TIP

God doesn't always give us what we *want*, but He always gives us what we *need*. So thank Him every day for looking after you.

Welcome, God

There are all sorts of ways to spend your time.

Unscramble the letters to find a list of hobbies, activities and jobs to be done:

What do you do...

...after school? **KWHOMER** _____

...with television? **TCHWA** _____

...on a bike? **ERDI** _____

...with a book? **ADRE** _____

...in a pool or the sea? **MISW** _____

...when the house is dirty? **ANCLE** _____

...with needles and wool? **TINK** _____

...with a football? **KKCI** _____

...with a needle and thread? **WSE** _____

...with crayons? **ROOLUC** _____

Answers on page 33

PRAY

God, thank You that I can spend my time in so many different ways. Whether it's a work day or a play day, please be with me and be part of everything I do. Amen.

TOPZ TIP

No matter how you spend each day, every morning, invite God to join you!

Prayer is for life!

"Have you heard people talk about 'lifestyles'? They mean different ways of living life. Some people have a 'nautical' lifestyle – that means they live near the sea and go out on boats a lot. Some people have a 'creative' lifestyle and spend time making things or writing things or painting things."

"Then there's the sporty lifestyle, where you just love doing sport. The more the better!"

The lifestyle God wants us to have is one that's full to the brim with prayer! God wants us to look forward to spending time with Him. He wants us to get excited about telling Him what's going on and what we're up to. He wants us to thank Him for every good thing we have and every good thing that happens. He wants to be there for us when things are hard and to hear exactly how we're feeling – because when we talk to Him, He can step in and help.

"God can be a part of everything we do. He wants to share each day with us! And when we talk to Him wherever we are, whatever we're doing, and invite Him in – it puts a big smile all over His face!"

PRAY

God, You created the enormous universe, yet You still want to hear from tiny me. That's awesome! Thank You. Amen.